Original title:
The Thorn and the Bard

Copyright © 2025 Creative Arts Management OÜ
All rights reserved.

Author: Rosalie Bradford
ISBN HARDBACK: 978-1-80566-730-8
ISBN PAPERBACK: 978-1-80566-859-6

## Lyrical Aftermaths of the Bloom

In a garden where giggles grow,
Petals dance with a funny show.
A gopher sings with a wiggly sway,
While daisies chuckle about their day.

A cactus wearing a comical grin,
Tells tales of time in the sun and din.
The bees buzz loud, but with a twist,
In such sweet chaos, no bloom is missed.

Frogs in bow ties leap with flair,
While butterflies toss their colored hair.
With each spin and flap, a laugh erupts,
Nature's chorus has all lives disrupted.

So here's to the blooms, with their quirky charms,
And the mirthful creatures with all their balms.
In this floral fiesta, joy we'll plume,
As we dance through the lyrical aftermaths of bloom.

## Where Roses Fear to Tread

In a garden where roses lie,
They sip tea and wave goodbye.
With petals soft and a snooty air,
They scorn all who don't play fair.

A dandelion spins a tall tale,
Of how it once sailed on a gale.
But when thorns start to dance nearby,
Even the posies learn to fly.

Underneath the sun's bright glare,
Petunias plot with less despair.
While daisies giggle, quite absurd,
At thorns who can't quite be heard.

The roses blush, they can't deny,
Their sharpness is just a little shy.
As laughter weaves through fragrant heads,
In the wacky world where laughter spreads.

## Thorns in the Garden of Whispers

In whispers soft, the thorns conspire,
With secrets shared that don't retire.
A daisy swears it's all a game,
While thorns just poke and shift the blame.

The garden gossips in a hush,
While cacti watch with a snarky blush.
Who knew that pricks could bring such cheer?
In this place, all smiles disappear.

A nettle stands with quite a flair,
While teasing roses, unaware.
They break into a jesty fight,
In a mishap that sparks delight.

So gardens bloom with giggles bright,
With thorny laughter, pure delight.
Forget the rules, let chaos reign,
For humor grows amid the pain.

## Secrets of the Sauntering Poet

A poet strolled through tangled vines,
With ink-stained hands and wobbly lines.
He laughed aloud at each bizarre,
For every thorn was a funny scar.

With every step, a pun would rise,
As humor danced 'neath sunny skies.
He wrote of thorns that claimed a prize,
And tricked the bees with crafty lies.

In shadows deep where secrets lay,
The poet sauntered on his way.
He spun tales of wit and jest,
Finding funny in every quest.

And so he wandered, pen in hand,
Transforming thorns to lover's band.
Where laughter echoes through the night,
And prickly tales bring pure delight.

## The Barbed Elegy

In barbed wire fencings where shadows sway,
A poet scribbled in a pun-filled way.
With twists and quirks upon his page,
He penned an ode to the thorny stage.

With every line a chuckle spun,
The thorns rolled laughter just for fun.
A clash of humor in green attire,
Where stitches coiled with floral fire.

The barbed elegy, quite absurd,
Left no listener untouched or stirred.
With thorns that pricked the velvet breeze,
Making merry with effortless ease.

So join the dance of jab and jab,
In gardens where giggles dub and blab.
For every thorn has a story to tell,
In the laughable, prickly echoing well.

## The Dance Between Joy and Pain

In the garden of woes, a jester pranced,
Tripping on petals, he laughed, he danced.
With a grin so wide, he stumbled in glee,
Whispering secrets to the buzzing bee.

Joy threw a party, pain brought the snacks,
With a cake of confusion, topped with some cracks.
Together they twirled, like partners in crime,
Tickling the fates, they danced out of time.

**Letters Laced in Thorny Texts.**

I penned my love with thorns on the page,
Each word a giggle, each line a stage.
Messages tangled like vines in the breeze,
Whispering riddles that only tease.

With a wink and a nod, I sent it away,
Dressed in mischief to brighten the day.
But perhaps I'll add a line that's sweet,
To soften the blow where twisters meet.

## Whispers of the Rose

A rose opened wide with a chuckle so bright,
Spitting out petals in a quixotic flight.
"Come dance with the thorns," it teased with a grin,
"Let's make a fuss and invite all the spin!"

But be wary," it warned, "of the prickles, my friend,
They tickle the toes but might start to offend."
With laughter they spun, what a whimsical fight,
As the thorns sang their songs, in the soft summer light.

## Echoes in the Gloom

In the shade of the gloom, a riddle took flight,
Echoes of laughter mingled with fright.
A surprisingly jolly, yet thorny old tree,
Chortled to shadows, "Come sit here with me!"

"Life's but a jest, with jabs and with jives,
The laughter is sharp, but it surely survives.
With a wink to the night and a hop to the day,
Let's poke fun at our troubles, come join in the play!"

## The Unkindest Cuts

A cactus pricked the poet's foot,
He danced around in quite the suit.
With every step, a new lament,
His verses now—quite different bent.

A squirrel laughed from yonder tree,
"Oh, poet friend, do do not flee!
Wear shoes, my lad, or else you'll find,
Your rhymes may turn to woes unkind!"

## Reverberations in an Untended Plot

In gardens wild, where weeds do thrive,
The bard composed, feeling alive.
But every tale, a twisty fight,
For bees mistook him for a light!

His lines got tangled, like the vines,
And laughter echoed through designs.
"Oh woe!" he cried, "I'm quite a mess,
I'd rather sing of love, no stress!"

## **Cries of a Bard Unbound**

A lonely bard with words so new,
Cried out to skies a bright blue hue.
He tripped on chords and rhymes absurd,
"Excuse my plight!" was all he heard.

With laughter bouncing off the walls,
He crafted songs of baseballs and falls.
His hopes were high, his hat askew,
And all his woes became a stew!

## Petals in the Wind's Grasp

A poet tossed his words like leaves,
But petals danced and played tricks, thieves!
They swirled around, quite in a whirl,
The bard just sighed, "Oh what a curl!"

With every breeze, his stanzas flew,
Each line, it seemed, had lost its dew.
"Come back!" he yelled, "Don't go astray!
I need you all for my next play!"

## Chronicles of Daisies and Thorns

In a garden where daisies play,
Thorns joke about in a light ballet.
Petals swish, while prickles pounce,
Laughter blooms with each little flounce.

The daisies giggle, a merry tune,
While thorns roll their eyes, quite immune.
"Get off my stem!" the daisies shout,
But thorns just chuckle and dance about.

A bee buzzes in with a happy dance,
"Who needs trouble? Let's take a chance!"
With a twist and a twirl, they all start to sing,
In the land of flowers, it's a jolly fling.

So if you step in this garden of cheer,
Watch out for thorns—they've got quite the sneer.
But with daisies galore, it's hard to lose,
Just laugh with the thorns, or you might get bruised.

## The Poet's Heart in a Bed of Roses

Amidst the roses, a poet sat,
With thoughts of rhymes and his favorite hat.
But petals giggled and thorns took a poke,
As the lines got tangled, what a funny joke!

He scribbled verses, but they slipped away,
Dodging his quill like a game of tag play.
"Dear roses, sit still!" he laughed in despair,
But even the buds were too busy to care.

His heart skipped beats like a flustered bird,
As thorns whispered secrets, absurd and unheard.
"Oh, dear poet, it's a raucous affair,
You write us a ballad, we'll tease you with flair!"

With a wink and a chuckle, he joined in the fun,
Penning odd verses till the day was done.
In a bed of blooms, he found such delight,
For laughter and poetry danced in the night.

## Stitched in Silence, Inked in Blood

In a corner dark, where secrets sleep,
A patchwork of tales begins to creep.
Stitches of laughter, sewn with delight,
Yet thorns poke sharply, oh what a sight!

The poet grins, with a wink and a nod,
Crafting his phrases, unbothered, but awed.
Each prick a reminder of stories to weave,
Inked with the memories that he can't believe.

While silence hums a deep, earnest tune,
Prickly conspirators plot to out-moon.
With mischievous whispers and gallant intent,
They tumble through verses, by laughter unbent.

So here in the shadows, the fun shall arise,
With stitches of humor, the poet complies.
Inked in good cheer, his heart learns to soar,
As thorns crack a smile—now, who could ask for more?

## Echoes of Sorrow and Song

In a valley where echoes sing low,
Sorrow and song hold a peculiar glow.
Thorns find a tune that's cheeky and bright,
While daisies watch on, laughing outright.

A troubadour plucks strings with a frown,
'Cause thorns have a penchant for pulling him down.
"Sing us a ballad!" the blossoms all call,
While the poet just stumbles, about to fall.

With every note, a comical clash,
As thorns shimmy close and create a splash.
Sorrow meets laughter in curious twirls,
While echoes of giggles fly out like swirls.

At dusk, they all gather, a musically fond
Affair of motley, a harmonious bond.
In the play of the night, sweet woe knows to scoff,
For in joy's wild embrace, they all laugh and loft!

## Scribe of the Weeping Rose

A pen in hand, I whip and twirl,
It's harder than a squirrel's whirl.
Each word I write, a tickled beast,
With giggles loud, my joys released.

But thorns do bite, oh what a scene,
While writing jests, my fingers keen.
A paper cut, a man's worst fate,
I laugh and scribble—ain't this great?

Each stanza trips, it jibes and jolts,
Like dancing with the craziest vaults.
Yet still I pen, with ink in streams,
For life's a jest, or so it seems!

So here I am, the weeping scribe,
With thoughts so funky, they can't describe.
Let laughter flow, and thorns be tamed,
In this wild world, I'm never shamed.

## Chords from the Gritted Path

Strumming tunes on gravel roads,
With rhythm lost, my facon goads.
A song of hiccups, bumps, and scrapes,
My melody hails the thorniest shapes.

I hum a tune, then scratch my head,
What's this bizarre path I have tread?
My guitar laughs as my fingers miss,
The notes are here, but where's the bliss?

With each sharp chord, my heart does sing,
While thorns and giggles twirl in spring.
I dance alone, a circus show,
In funny shoes, I steal the glow!

Yet deep within, a secret lies,
The chords may jest, but still they rise.
Through laughter's lens, we forge and play,
On gritty paths, come what may.

## The Pain Beneath the Ink


A scribble here, a squiggle there,
With every stroke, a thorn to bear.
Inky fingers, oh such a plight,
But don't you fret; I'll write all night!

My coffee spills, it drips, it stains,
As laughter dances on my veins.
Each drop a joke, each blot a muse,
In the chaos, there's fun to choose.

Oh, pain you say? It pricks the skin,
But watch me spin, and take the win!
With every jab, a giggle tumbles,
Much like a cat with clumsy fumbles.

So ink is spilled and laughter flows,
Let's write a tale where humor grows.
For in the pain, we find the fun,
A twinkling jest, a life well-run.

## Songs Amongst the Thicket

In thickets wild where laughter hides,
A raucous song the forest guides.
With critters prancing, oh what a sight,
Their little jig ignites the night.

Each thorn that pricks becomes a joke,
As bushes quiver, the branches poke.
I sing along, with cheer sublime,
In nature's band, we dance in rhyme.

They croon a tune, I join the fun,
While twisty paths beneath us run.
Adventure stirs, in every flap,
Where thicket teases me to tap.

So let us play, with thorns embraced,
In joyous tunes, we're interlaced.
A symphony of giggles loud,
Amongst the thicket, we sing proud!

## Bard's Melodies and Prickly Paths

In a forest of giggles, a bard took a leap,
Carving tunes from the thickets, where secrets do creep.
Snagged by a bramble, he danced with despair,
Singing sweet serenades, while pulling at hair.

His lute strummed the laughter, the thorns made a show,
Poking and prodding, oh what a woe!
Yet every mishap turned sweet to the ear,
For pricks made him chuckle, and we cheered him near.

## Whispered Tales of Pain and Elegance

Beneath the soft whispers, elegance snoozed,
A bard with a quill, oh so nicely bruised.
He scribbled in circles, tales blooming with ache,
But laughter sprouted from every heartache.

With puns like sharp needles, he pricked through the gloom,
Turning tears into giggles with wit in full bloom.
An elegy wrapped in a jester's bright tune,
Every line like a thorn, yet we danced to its rune.

## Sonnet of Shadows and Splinters

In shadows of splinters, he wove out a verse,
A bard with a grin, through pain he did curse.
Each thorn was a riddle, a jest in disguise,
As he tackled his troubles with bright, saucy cries.

The audience chuckled, all pain transformed,
For laughter was magic, and thorns kept them warmed.
Splinters of humor, a play on the heart,
With wit like a double-edged sword as his art.

## **Ballad of Roses and Regrets**

In a garden of roses, a bard found his muse,
But the thorns, they were fickle, oh what could he choose?

He wrote of sweet blossoms with a twist in the stem,
Regrets like confetti, a whimsy for them.

Each petal a giggle, each thorn a sly poke,
As he tiptoed through laughter, with every stroke.
His ballad rang bright, though the pricks made a sound,
Bringing smiles instead of the frowns that abound.

# The Jagged Cacophony of Life

In a garden overgrown, weeds play their tune,
Curly plants dance wildly, under the moon.
Frogs wear top hats, croaking their spree,
While ants throw a party, sipping sweet tea.

Pigeons on rooftops gossip and caw,
Debating the best way to avoid the law.
Squirrels in bow ties scamper and dart,
While dandelions plot to steal every heart.

A snail on a mission, slow but so wise,
Outruns a rabbit with well-laid lies.
The sun takes a bow, ducks behind trees,
As laughter erupts with the evening breeze.

In life's jagged song, we stumble and trip,
Yet dance on the notes of this quirky script.
With pokes and with prods, it's a comical ride,
Through the chaos of nature, let humor abide.

## **Serpentines of Love and Lament**

Once a rose wooed a thistle in bloom,
Said, 'Your prickles add character, not doom!'
They tangoed through gardens, lost in their jest,
Each thorn a reminder of love's playful quest.

A snail serenades, his shell all aglow,
With verses that twinkle, though moves very slow.
The ladybugs chuckle, as they form a line,
Swaying to rhythms of the heart's whimsy design.

Yet autumn winds howl, causing petals to cry,
As heart-shaped leaves flutter from branches nearby.
But love finds a way among gossiping flowers,
In serpentines winding through the dusk's final hours.

For every lament, a chuckle arrives,
In gardens where humor and heartbreak survive.
With blooms and with thorns, we dance through the night,

In this wild, tangled web, love feels just right.

## Harmonies Lost Among the Stalks

A chorus of plants, all shouting their songs,
Sing of the mishaps where each one belongs.
The corn does a jig, the beans boast and brag,
While carrots peek out, waving their rag.

But then comes a breeze, it rustles the leaves,
A tumble of giggles, as everyone grieves.
The tomatoes roll over, their cheeks all aglow,
As cucumbers chuckle, 'Oh, look at the show!'

With roots intertwined, the weeds stir the pot,
'Who invited the slugs?' giggled one little tot.
The daisies chime in, a whimsical flare,
As laughter erupts in the balmy warm air.

Though harmonies falter, and melodies crash,
In the garden of life, we find joy in a splash.
With blooms in a twist, and each tale anew,
We sow seeds of laughter, well into the blue.

## The Parable of Points and Pearls

A pointy prickly plant told tales at dawn,
Of pearls that travel, so sleek and withdrawn.
"I might be a headache, a poke in the side,
But pearls wear the crown, and I shall abide!"

The points and the pearls had a dance-offs that day,
The prickly ones strutted, while the shiny ones sway.
With petals for skirts and seeds in their hair,
Laughter erupted, a whimsical air.

But pearls turned to points and thought they could shine,
In chaos they twisted, proclaiming, "We're fine!"
Yet those in the dirt, with their tangles and grime,
Giggled at pearls and their lost sense of time.

So in this grand tale, where humor does twirl,
Points find their charm, just like shines of a pearl.
Together they flourish, the rough and the sweet,
In this parable's dance, they find joy in their beat.

## Lament of the Prickled Heart

A heart so bold, with spikes to show,
When love comes near, it starts to grow.
But oh, the blush on my cheek ends fast,
For hugs become a thing of the past.

I wrote a note, it slipped from view,
Scribbled my love, but pricked my shoe.
So here I stand, with wounded pride,
A hopeful heart, yet can't abide.

In the garden of dreams, I surely tread,
With every step, I dance instead.
For laughter blooms where sorrow stings,
And in my rhymes, the giggle sings.

So heed this tale, of joy and pain,
In love's wild game, we all are slain.
With prickles sharp, we bravely play,
And find the fun in every fray.

## A Melody in the Shadows

In shadows' dance, where secrets creep,
A strum of notes, that laughter keeps.
The ghost among the hedges laughs,
While writing songs of love's mishaps.

With every strum, a chord does tease,
The garden's mess hides such expertise.
Yet when the moon begins to glow,
The tune turns wild; oh, what a show!

Around each thorn, a jest is spun,
A sassy tale of a love not won.
So spin me round, through petals and laughs,
In music's grasp, mischief drafts.

We dance beneath the weeping blooms,
With every twirl, chaos looms.
Yet in the fun, no hurt is felt,
For laughter's warmth is truly dealt.

## Petals in the Dust

Among the thorns, a soft petal dropped,
With laughter's ease, my worries were stopped.
For every bump on this winding road,
A chuckle's worth is shared and bestowed.

In fields of dust, we twirl and spin,
With quirky moves and silly grins.
Each petal lost, a tale to tell,
Of joyous blunders that cast our spell.

So gather 'round, ye prickle-toed mates,
Unpack your woes, let's lighten the fates.
For laughter blooms where shadows play,
In the garden of mishaps, we'll sway.

And as we roam through this floral maze,
With giggles and joy, we'll earn our praise.
Amidst the dust and prickles we find,
Life's sweetest moments, joyfully blind.

## Ballad of the Bitter Stem

In a garden bright, a jest unfolds,
The bitter stem, with antics bold.
He sways and swerves, a pompous show,
Unruly charm, a wry hello.

With every poke, he claims his right,
To dance alone, a comical sight.
Yet laughter sprouts from every prick,
In the realm of love, he's quite the trick!

The blossoms giggle, the branches sway,
Onlookers chuckle at his display.
For in his bitterness, a truth shines bright,
That love offends, but warms the night.

So raise a glass to the thorny tale,
Of sweet rebellion, we shall prevail.
With silly laughs, we'll all partake,
In the ballad of life, we'll never break.

## The Silent Strains of Sorrow

The minstrel played a tune so sly,
But the notes flew off to kiss the sky.
His lute was out of tune, oh dear,
It sounded more like a goat in fear.

With every pluck, a sneeze would come,
The audience giggled, not feeling glum.
He juggled keys, lost track of time,
The laughs erupted, oh what a rhyme!

His songs of woe turned into jest,
He sang of lost socks and birdie nests.
The tale of a hat, blown by the breeze,
Left all in fits, brought to their knees.

So the bard's sorrow turned bright and cheery,
With laughter shared, the hearts grew leery.
In tears of joy, the crowd would sway,
And mournful songs turned to a cabaret!

## Dreams Entangled in Thorns

In a garden lush, dreams took a twist,
Thorns caught laughter, none could resist.
A jester danced, with petals in hand,
Slipping and sliding, in this bright land.

He tripped on a bramble, fell with a squeal,
"Is this a dream or is it real?"
The roses laughed, petals a-flight,
While the thorns whispered, "What a sight!"

As he rolled in the grass with glee galore,
His crown of roses fell with a roar.
The thorns conspired with vibrant foes,
"Just a jest, dear bard, where laughter grows!"

A serenade sung to the moon so bright,
With shadows dancing in the silver light.
Caught in the thicket, they howled and sung,
Making a tune that forever sprung!

## The Mournful Blossomer

There once bloomed a flower, oh so blue,
But every day, it sneezed, too true!
With every petal, pollen near,
It wailed out loud, "Please lend me an ear!"

The bees would buzz, perplexed and slow,
"Why do you mourn?" they wished to know.
The flower replied, in tones of despair,
"I've lost my sunshine, it's just not fair!"

So the bard strummed a funny little tune,
Promised to bring back the sun by noon.
He wore a bright hat, with feathers so tall,
The flower giggled, "I'm having a ball!"

With laughter and joy, the flower did cheer,
For in happy moments, there's nothing to fear.
He bloomed even brighter, amidst the jest,
And finally felt like he'd passed the test!

## **Inked in Dried Sorrow**

A poet sat, with ink-stained hands,
He wrote of woes across the lands.
Each verse he penned, dripped with despair,
But found it funny, his woes to share.

In every stanza, a joke slipped through,
"Oh, woe is me!" he'd sing anew.
Yet laughter bubbled where sadness thrived,
For the sadder the tale, the funnier it arrived!

His quill took flight like a bird on a spree,
Scribbling tales of lost socks with glee.
"The world's a stage, with chaos to spare,
Let's dance in the rain with no cares to wear!"

So in his heart, a chuckle grew wide,
Through inked sorrow, joy did abide.
His verses became a rollicking spree,
And every thorn brought a giggle, you see!

## Epistles from a Barbed Heart

In a garden where roses can poke,
A poet sat laughing, not a word he spoke.
His quill was a thorn, ink dripping in jest,
Each letter he'd write put his patience to test.

With a giggle he penned, 'Oh, love, how you sting!'
But the heart sings a tune that only fools bring.
He mailed off his woes with a wink and a cheer,
For laughter and heartache can dwell ever near.

## Words that Cut

A wordsmith once claimed he had daggers for words,
He'd slice through the silence, like thorns from the birds.
With a chuckle, he prattled, 'What's sharp may be sweet,'
He winked at the crowd, they all took a seat.

'You say I'm a thorn? I prefer cactus!'
He laughed as they gasped, 'Oh dear, that's quactu-ous!'
For words can be witty, like puns in the night,
Each jab in his verses brought chuckles and fright.

## Songs that Heal

In a grove where the music was pricked by the thorns,
A minstrel sang sharply, yet hearts weren't torn.
With a grin on his face and a lute on his knee,
He strummed all the notes like a buzzing bee.

'Every cut has a cure in the ballads I croon,'
He'd sing with a flair, under mischief's soft moon.
His songs floated freely, a tickle and tease,
In the garden of heartache, it's laughter that frees.

## The Frailty of Flowers and Words

In the meadows where daisies wore crowns of delight,
The poet remarked on their soft, fluffy plight.
'Why do we worry? Each bloom has its spines,
They're fragile but fierce, like my best punchline!'

With petals like whispers, they danced in the breeze,
And the verses he crafted made even thorns sneeze.
For laughter is flowery, a jest on each petal,
Stumbling through seriousness, life's eccentric medal.

## Breezes Through a Garden of Barbs

Through gardens of mischief the breezes would weave,
Amongst jokes and barbs, laughter up their sleeve.
A jester once said, as he juggled the blooms,
'In this patch, my friends, we harvest the glooms.'

With each gust of humor, the thorns cracked a smile,
Turning prickles to giggles, they stayed for a while.
In the tale that we tell, it's the joy that we keep,
For even sharp moments can gentle the leap.

## A Serenade for the Weary Heart

In a garden of laughter, I stumbled with pride,
A flowerpot's winking, oh what a ride!
The sun was a jester, just teasing the bees,
While squirrels in tuxedos danced with such ease.

But clouds were a prankster, a sprinkle of rain,
The daisies looked up, all giggles and bane.
They swayed to the music of puddles so wide,
As I tripped on a root, my joy turned to glide.

The breeze told a secret, a tale of delight,
Of butterflies giggling, taking their flight.
So I laughed with the flowers, my worries away,
In a serenade sweet, I found humor's bouquet.

So here's to the folly, the funny and light,
In the garden of heart, let laughter ignite!
With each prick and each poke, a smile I'll impart,
For joy blooms most brightly in a weary heart.

## **Prickles in the Poetry**

Oh, the poems I scribble are full of surprise,
With quills made of thorns and mischief in eyes.
My verses they dance, like hedgehogs in shoes,
Prickles in stanzas, oh what do I choose?

With laughter I pen, but the ink sometimes squirts,
A sonnet gone rogue, how it truly flirts.
Rhymes tangle like vines, in a wild thicket,
Words poke at my heart, but I laugh and I pick it.

A haiku enchanted, I crafted with glee,
But the twist was a cactus, oh woe is me!
Each line that I wrote brought a chuckle, a hiss,
In the prickles of poetry, I found bliss.

So beware of the quills when you traverse my verse,
For laughter and tangles might make it a curse.
Yet I'll share my sweet humor, oh what a show,
In the prickles of poetry, let giggles grow!

## The Scribe's Sorrow in Bloom

In a booth of a café, I scribble and sigh,
A mug of cold coffee, a cupcake gone by.
My words are like daisies that wrinkle and fade,
Yet they're dancing with sorrow, a light masquerade.

The napkin's a canvas, my heart's on display,
Filling blank spaces with what I can say.
But each time I write, my ideas go poof,
Like a rogue little fairy with no lasting proof.

Yet laughter's a blossom that starts to unfold,
In the ink of my sorrow, sweet memories are told.
Each petal a giggle, each stem echoes bright,
As I turn my misfortune into sheer delight.

So raise up a glass to the tales that we weave,
In the scribe's little garden, there's always reprieve.
In humor and heartache, they twist and they bloom,
For the sorrow I carry transforms into room.

## Echoing Whispers of Conflict

In the realm of my musings, a spat starts to brew,
Two poets in laughter, debating their view.
One claims that the pen should always be might,
While the other demands that the joke takes its flight.

With thorns wrapped in humor, they nudge and they jest,
As rhymes turn to jousts in their feathery quest.
Each line they declare, like a cupcake with sprinkles,
A battle for sanity, confusion in twinkles.

But in echoes of laughter, their differences fade,
As they scribble their stories, a friendship is made.
The conflict was silly, just whims in the air,
Like dueling with pillows, who really would care?

So raise up your glasses, let laughter abound,
For in whispers of conflict, friendship is found.
In the comedy of words, let joy be released,
As we dance through our verses, united at least!

## **Ballad Under the Thorny Canopy**

In a garden where roses do sing,
A hedgehog danced, dreaming of spring.
With a top hat and shoes, oh so bright,
He wobbled and jiggled until late at night.

A snail wearing shades, quite the sight,
Joined in the fun, moving with slight.
They twirled with joy, oh what a mess,
In a thorny embrace, they felt no stress.

## Melancholy of the Gilded Leaf

A leaf fell down, shimmering gold,
It sighed with tales that never get old.
"Why am I cast aside with a frown?"
Asked the leaf as it spun towards the ground.

A bee with a buzz, made it his throne,
"You're lovely, dear leaf, though you moan!"
They laughed till the dusk began to creep,
In a world of chatter, no time for sleep.

## Peddler of Worn-out Verses

A jester strolled, with a grin so wide,
Selling rhymes in a capricious tide.
"Get your verses! New and used!"
He yelled with glee, slightly confused.

A line for a coin, a rhyme for a laugh,
He questioned his craft, then took a gaff.
"A pun for your heart, a joke for your soul!"
His silly charisma made everyone whole.

## **Prickles of Memory**

In the thicket where mischief does lurk,
A hedgehog reminisced of his quirky work.
He pranced on the path, with style and flair,
Sharing old tales just to lighten the air.

From tangles of branches to giggles at noon,
Every prickly memory hummed a tune.
"Oh, the joy of a joke that won't fade away!"
As they laughed at the thorns of yesterday.

## Singed Words of Winter's Embrace

In a frostbitten nook, with a quill in hand,
A poet once tripped over ice so grand.
His ink froze in place, words caught in the chill,
He chuckled and mused, 'What a winter thrill!'

With snowflakes that danced, his thoughts took flight,
They tumbled like laughter, pure delight.
But each time he'd write, his fingers would freeze,
'This winter's a prankster; oh, if you please!'

A squirrel, quite cheeky, stole his warm tea,
With a sip and a twirl, it shouted with glee.
'This brew is too hot, but it's mine now, see?'
The poet just laughed, said, 'Make merry, dear tree!'

So if you find ink in a snow-laden world,
Remember the bard and the antics unfurled.
For winter might chill, but laughter beats frost,
In the heart of the poet, no joy shall be lost.

## The Perilous Tale of Blooming Hearts

In a garden so bright, with flowers so bold,
A dandelion whispered, 'Be careful, I'm told!'
When love blooms too fast, it can head south, too,
And leave you with nothing but the wish of a stew.

A rose thought it cute to swoon and to sway,
But thorns jabbed a wink, 'Let's not play this way!'
With petals a-quiver, they laughed in disdain,
'If love's a game, then we all feel the pain!'

The lilies declared, 'We will eat from the sky,'
While daisies giggled, 'Oh my, oh my!'
With each bobbing head, their secrets they shared,
In a world full of blooms, who truly has dared?

So heed well the whims of affection's sweet art,
The blooming of love is a festival of heart.
Yet look for the thorns, as you wander in cheer,
For the funny and the fierce go hand in hand here!

## Echoes of a Wounded Muse

In a tavern so loud, with laughter and drink,
A muse lost her foot, gave her ankle a wink.
She tripped on a rhyme, fell into the stew,
Said, 'Next time I'll focus on something brand new!'

The bards in the corner let out a loud cheer,
'Oh muse, you're our star, don't you disappear!'
With goblets held high, they sang to her grace,
Though she got stuck, it was all just a chase.

With each clumsy tumble, a story unfurled,
Of muses with bruises in a whimsical world.
They played silly games with ink and some rhyme,
Turning misfortunes into comedic crime.

So raise up your glass, here's a toast to the fall!
For echoes of laughter can brighten it all.
When muses get wounded, let joy take the lead,
In the heart of mischief, true art is conceived!

## The Ballad of Wounded Petals

In a meadow of colors, where laughter rang bright,
Petals played dress-up, oh what a sight!
The daisies wore hats, while the tulips sang loud,
But a gust of wind came and swirled up the crowd.

A sunflower slipped, in her oversized shade,
Landed smack down, oh what a cascade!
'I'm blooming in style, can't anyone see?'
As petals were tangled in glorious glee.

The dandelions giggled, rolling in mirth,
'Just look at our friend, the queen of the turf!'
With every mishap, laughter echoed around,
In a garden of whimsy, joy always is found.

So remember, dear friends, as you dance with the breeze,
Life is a petal, with trials and tease.
For laughter will bloom in the strangest of ways,
In the heart of a flower, the joy always stays.

## A Chorus of Bittersweet Yearning

In a garden of mischief, a sprout does grow,
With giggles and snickers, in sunlight's glow.
Beneath its bright petals, a secret doth hide,
A prankster's ambition, it cannot abide.

Oh, the dance of the bees, with a wink and a sting,
They twirl and they tumble, oh what joy they bring!
But one little jab, and you'll stumble and trip,
It's all in good fun, though it may make you flip.

Laughter erupts at the sight of the thorns,
A party of petals in wild, raucous forms.
They tease and they tumble, in a riotous jest,
All in the name of this curious quest.

So raise up a glass to the thorns with a cheer,
For every sharp poke brings the laughter near.
In this garden of folly, we find what is true,
A humor immortal, a joy ever new.

## The Weaving of Pain and Poetry

A poet once sat with his quill and his dream,
Grumbling 'bout life, he let out a scream.
With ink like a thorn, on the page it did spread,
Painting his heartache, his humor instead.

In his verses, he chuckled at troubles so small,
A yelp from the thorns, then a laugh from us all.
Each line a tightrope, a whimsical dance,
Balancing sorrow and a comical chance.

He tangled his thoughts in a web spun with glee,
Creating a tapestry for all who could see.
And yet, with each stitch, a prick of the pain,
A reminder that laughter can sometimes feel vain.

So let us all gather, with ink-stained delight,
In the shadows of thorns, we'll take wing in flight.
For weaving our woes with a wink and a grin,
Brings forth all the laughter that lies deep within.

## Rhymes of the Harsh Landscape

Amidst rugged mountains, where thorns stand tall,
A jester once tripped, sending laughter to all.
His songs filled with jabs, like a thorn in his side,
Yet still he pressed on, with joy as his guide.

The rocks would chuckle, 'neath skies painted gray,
As he sang to the clouds, on this jolly ballet.
Every tumble and fall, he made into verse,
With a grin on his face, never fearful of worse.

For nature, it teases with sharp edges and wit,
Each thorn like a punchline, just a bit of a hit.
He danced on the ridges, in poetic embrace,
Finding joy in the pain, in this rugged place.

So let us convene in a land full of jest,
Where prickers and giggles both know they are blessed.
With rhymes of the harsh and the sweet intertwine,
We laugh at the thorns, and our spirits align.

## Pensive Petals of Memory

In a field full of blossoms, a ponderous thought,
A petal remembered the battles it fought.
With whispers of laughter, it danced in the air,
Recalling past pricks, yet still feeling fair.

With nostalgia in bloom, it twirled with delight,
Sharing tales of the thorns that gave such a fright.
"Oh, stings were abundant, but oh what a show,
Life's jokes come unbidden, like rain with a glow!"

The petals all giggled, as thorns licked their brims,
In the garden of memory, their laughter brims.
Each bloom knows the secrets of growing with glee,
Even after the pricks, we're still wild and free.

So gather your petals, your stories of cheer,
For each thorn that we meet teaches us to endear.
In the dance of remembrance, we grow hand in hand,
Finding joy in the thorns, in this whimsical land.

## The Gnarl of Dreams

In a garden of giggles, I found my way,
A prickly little path where the roses play.
But watch your step, dear friend, it's not quite right,
Those giggling blooms bloom mostly at night.

I tripped over laughter, fell into a joke,
The thorns whispered secrets, poked fun like a poke.
With every snicker, the night danced with glee,
A magical mess, just waiting for me.

I chased after sunbeams, through shadows of fun,
Where thickets were ticklish, and pranks were well done.
Even the crickets were chuckling around,
As I juggled my shoes till they fell to the ground.

So here's to the thorns, in their quirky attire,
They tickle my senses, igniting a fire.
With each turn of fate, a new jest I glean,
In this wacky old garden, a fool's never seen.

## Verse from the Briar's Edge

At the edge of a briar, I planted a rhyme,
With thorns on the bushes like scribbles in time.
The words pricked my fingers, oh what a delight,
As I danced on the edge in the fading twilight.

A bard with a banjo, strumming away,
Sang songs to the stars, in a hilarious way.
The thorns kept on jabbing, he laughed in their face,
"It's a fine time for jesting, let's cherish this place!"

While the bugs threw confetti, all dancing about,
The thorns twisted tales, sparking laughter and doubt.
With each note that echoed, they swayed to the tune,
As the moon took a bow, and the night turned to swoon.

So let's toast to the thorns, those fellows so bold,
Who know how to jest, and spin stories from old.
In the heart of the briar, where laughter ignites,
The joy of the words brings our humor to heights.

## The Enigma of Thorns

In the web of the weeds, a riddle appears,
With thorns made of giggles that twinkle like cheers.
They whisper their puzzles, a jester's delight,
Each point's a pinprick of humor so bright.

A desert of daisies, with a thistle or two,
Made a party of pranks where the wildflowers grew.
I asked for a clue, but the thorns played along,
Tickling my ear with a mischievous song.

With every sharp comment, they jived in the breeze,
A dance of confusion, they brought me to knees.
The enigma unraveled, as I finally saw,
Every twist of their humor was a marvelous flaw.

So ponder the prickle, let laughter take wing,
In a land where the thorns have the sharpest of sting.
For in jest there's a wisdom wrapped tight with a thorn,
In the dance of the edge, where all folly is born.

## Symphony of Silence and Sorrow

In a quiet glade where the thorns love to hide,
I heard a strange symphony, accompanied by pride.
With notes made of whispers and rhymes wrapped in care,
A plush little concert held high in the air.

The thorns played the strings, plucked laughter with ease,
While shadows danced gently, inspired by the breeze.
And sorrow, a jester, wore a hat of delight,
Each tear became music in the stillness of night.

"We're thorny and proud!" the ensemble declared,
With snickers and chirps, they were fully ensnared.
A comedic overture that tugged at my heart,
In the silence of sorrow, the comedy starts.

So listen, dear friend, to the thorns' merry tune,
In this odd little world, where they croon to the moon.
For laughter and silence can dance hand in hand,
Creating a symphony across this strange land.

## **Verses Woven in Briars**

In a garden of jests, where roses grow,
A poet slipped on a root, what a show!
He laughed as he tumbled, with thorns in his hair,
Said, "Words may be sharp, but so is my flair!"

With petals for pillows, he dreamt of his fame,
While nettles and snickers played a wild game.
He penned down his woes, ink dripped from his pen,
"Next time I'll sit, I'll stick to my den!"

A bee stole his thoughts, buzzing loud in the air,
He whispered, "Dear friend, don't you dare take my spare!"
Yet out of the tussle, a joke bloomed so bright,
A thorny tail of laughter filled the night.

Thus, here is the tale of a poet so bold,
Who found every ouch had a story to mold.
For in prickly moments, delight can be found,
In mischief and marvels that spin all around.

## Ode to the Hurt and the Muse

Amidst the green weeds, a muse took its flight,
Tickled by thorns in the dim, dusky light.
With ink splattered pages from trips gone awry,
She giggled and tumbled, and oh my, oh my!

"Dear poet," she said, "it's a riot, you see,
Your rhymes are all tangled, much like this old tree!"
Yet words flowed like honey from laughter so sweet,
As they danced in the air like a scrap of old sheet.

The sap dripped like nectar from branches so high,
While poets' mishaps flew like clouds in the sky.
Each thorn a reminder of folly and fun,
In a garden of chaos, they basked in the sun.

So raise up a cup, let's toast to our schemes,
For the hurt and the muse weave the silliest dreams.
We stumble and trip, yet still find our way,
In the laughter of echoes where wordplay can sway.

## Fables of the Sharp and the Sweet

Once a jester pranced on a green, prickly lane,
With a grin on his face through the prickle and pain.
He tickled a cactus, yelped loud with delight,
Said, "Sharpness has flavor, just look at my plight!"

With tales of mischief, he gathered a crowd,
Each verse he recited made laughter quite loud.
Though barbs tried to snag him and thorns found their way,
He danced like a fool, come what may, come what may!

Each line was a patch, with a hint of sweet charm,
As he spun yarns of woe, yet none came to harm.
For laughter, my friends, is the nectar we crave,
Even sharp little pricks can make us all brave.

So cherish the thorns, and the chuckles they bring,
For the sharp and the sweet make the heart start to sing.
In a fable of giggles, the tale's always neat,
For joy can be found with each prick and each beat.

## Lament in a Garden of Needles

In the garden of needles, a bard felt quite grim,
He pricked his own finger while trying to swim.
"Why write when I bleed?" he exclaimed with dismay,
Yet the prickles just chuckled and rolled 'til the day.

Heartaches and agendas went bouncing about,
As he wrestled with verses that seemed all about.
"These sticks pinch my thoughts, how can I ever rhyme?"

Yet the laughter of nature made words feel sublime.

A sunflower twirled, oh so tall and so proud,
It whispered, "Dear bard, you're part of the crowd!"
So he laughed at his plight, with a wince and a cheer,
Found joys in the jabs and the jests that were near.

So here's to the ouchies, the ticks and the snags,
They teach us to grin, to giggle, and brag.
In a prickly old garden, where hilarity thrives,
The bard found his heart and learned how to jive.

## Tales of the Crimson Thorn

In the garden where laughter grows,
A thorn pricked the poet's toes.
He leaped and danced with all his might,
To chase the pesky bug that took flight.

Bards in bushes tell tales so grand,
Of roses that fought back, oh so planned.
With petals fierce and thorns aglow,
They danced a jig, each brave and slow.

A tart young sprout, a funny sight,
Wrestled with weeds in a comedic fight.
The flora chuckled, roots shook with glee,
As blooms paraded, wild and free.

And in the end, all flowers sang,
Of mishaps, laughter, and the joy they bring.
For in this patch where jokes are born,
Every thorn has its tale, well worn.

## Heartstrings of Gnarled Roots

Deep in the soil, where shadows play,
Roots twist and turn, in a humorous way.
They tell the story of a bard's bad aim,
Who tripped on a root, oh what a shame!

With a twang and a snap, his lute took flight,
Melody mixed with the roots' delight.
The shrubs laughed loud, their leaves a-quiver,
As tunes took turns, setting hearts to shiver.

Gnarled and twisted, like jokes that unfold,
The roots told secrets, both funny and bold.
A giggling vine tangled in woe,
Wrapped 'round the bard's leg, oh no!

But him, a chuckle, let nothing be grim,
For every awkward story gave life a whim.
In laughter and roots, they found their pride,
A symphony of joy forever wide.

## The Poet's Wounded Flute

A flute on a mission, to serenade the night,
But a thorn took its toll, much to its fright.
With every note, a painful squeak,
Instead of a song, it gave a shriek!

The poet puzzled, what could it be?
A cranky old flute, so stubborn and free.
He played a tune that caused a ruckus,
And danced with the flowers in riotous focus!

The grass giggled, "Oh look at that!"
As the bard's nimble feet went splat!
With every slip, the laughter soared,
As nature joined in, their fun restored.

But in the end, the flute found its sound,
With a little help from the giggles around.
A melody precious, from chaos set free,
In the heart of the garden, where all could see.

## Carnations in the Briar Patch

Carnations danced in a briar's embrace,
A tangle of petals in a flowery race.
With thorns all around, they twirled and spun,
In a patch full of laughter, they shone like the sun.

One flower slipped, went tumbling down,
Rolling in laughter, it looked like a clown.
The briars chuckled, "Ouch! That's absurd!"
As the carnation fluffed, undeterred.

A small bug passed, a curious sight,
Joined in the fun, danced left and right.
With each little stumble, the blooms sighed with glee,
Creating a banquet of silly esprit.

And when the sun set, in hues of delight,
The patch whispered stories to the night.
For in the dance of thorns and cheer,
Every flower knew, fun is near!

## Beneath Prickled Arches

Beneath the arch of thorns we sit,
A jester's cap, a snug fit.
With plucked flowers in our hair,
We dance on woes, without a care.

The prickle pokes, a friendly jab,
As laughter flows, we share the drab.
A bouncy ball of jest and glee,
Who knew thorns could set us free?

With every snag, a sly remark,
We laugh till night ignites the spark.
'Twas only twigs that brought us here,
We jest and laugh without a fear.

So here's a cheer to jests like these,
With prickers tickling at our knees.
In prickled arches, mirth resides,
Where humor blooms and joy abides.

## The Unplucked Strings of Fate

In tunes of chance, we strum along,
A chorus built from pluck and prong.
Unplucked strings, they twist and jig,
With fate's own hand, we dance a gig.

A violin made from a thistle's thorn,
Plays laughter notes till break of dawn.
Each note a tickle, every chord a jest,
In tangled tunes, we find our rest.

The violin sings, and we can't help,
To wiggle, jiggle, and do a yelp.
A merry tune that pricks the ear,
With laughter's echo ringing clear.

So strum away, dear friend of mine,
In thorns we find the perfect line.
With humor rich as ripened grapes,
We pluck the strings, and fate escapes.

## Evoking the Enigmatic

Oh, what a puzzle wrapped in fun,
In thorns we ponder, just begun.
A quirky riddle, full of cheer,
With every turn, we lose a tear.

Enigma dances in the light,
A mischief-maker, oh so bright.
Each twist and turn, a giggle waits,
A riddle served on silver plates.

No answer found, just silly grins,
As laughter echoes, love begins.
An enigma wrapped in our jest,
With every thorn, we're truly blessed.

So let's embrace the mystic flair,
With giggles bouncing through the air.
In thorns we craft the lightest jest,
Unraveling joy, we've come to rest.

## A Tangle of Verse and Vexation

In tangled lines where verses play,
A vexing time, but bright as day.
With every word, a twist, a turn,
The jester laughs; it's his to learn.

Oh, vexed emotions, spinning fast,
In tangled measures, echoes last.
We wrangle words like kittens wild,
Each phrase a jest from wisdom's child.

With every poke, we find our rhyme,
A playful dance through the sands of time.
In jointed jests, we weave our tale,
With thorns for laughs, we shall not fail.

So here's to verse and vexing plight,
We wiggle worms in the morning light.
In playful jests, though tangled still,
We find the gaps and laugh at will.

## Sorrow's Sweet Enchantment

In a garden where shy daisies hide,
A jester twirls with a grin so wide.
He trips on roots, but laughs, oh so spry,
While thorns poke the clouds in a dance up high.

His jingle hats, an odd mismatched pair,
Tangle with roses, a comical snare.
With every poke, he giggles anew,
Singing songs of mischief 'neath skies so blue.

Amidst the laughter, thorns plant their pride,
Yet the jester prances, arms open wide.
For every sweet thorn holds a tale to share,
In this whimsical realm, all frolic and dare.

As he tumbles through petals, he squeals with glee,
Who knew sharp little prickles could set him so free?
Each thorn a reminder, each laugh a delight,
In this garden of jesters, where day meets night.

## The Poet's Bitter Kiss

A poet once dreamed of love on a hill,
With roses adorning the place he sat still.
But every sweet promise left pricking surprise,
For the thorns shared secrets, unveiling their lies.

He penned with conviction, a ballad of woe,
Yet his ink spilled with laughter from tales not meant slow.
Each fluttering paper blew into a snag,
As the branches waved sharply, 'Don't let your heart lag!'


With lips stained in verse and a grin like a fool,
He kissed his quill hard, oh what an odd tool!
The thorns watched in glee, as they pricked at his pride,
In a dance of mischief, where hopes mostly hide.

Yet through tangled laughter, he spun tales of love,
With colors of madness unfurling above.
For a kiss can be bitter, but sweet is the rhyme,
As long as the thorns help him dance through the grime.

## Sonnet of Twilight's Grasp


When twilight drapes gently, the stage is set bright,
With mischief and laughter slipping into the night.
The thorns play their part, a comical plot,
As the bards weave their tales, both funny and hot.

A lute strums loudly, a jester appears,
He juggles with stars, tossing away fears.
With thorns on his forehead, a crown so bizarre,
He mocks the stern night, 'Come dance with the stars!'

As the sun gives a wink, and nods on the way,
The bards share their fortunes, all frayed by display.
Each word painted wild, with laughter and glee,
In this sonnet of twilight, so oddly carefree.

So gather round closely, and let your heart bask,
In the joy of the night, you shan't need to ask.
For the thorns may be sharp, but how light is the jest,
When laughter is sung, you'll find all is best.

## **Bards Beneath the Gnarly Tree**

Beneath the old tree with branches askew,
A band of bards gather, their mischief in view.
With laughter that echoes, they take off their hats,
For thorns speak their wisdom, as wise as the cats.

One bard sings of thunder, while another of rain,
Each word entwined with a chuckle and strain.
The thorns laugh along, poking fun in the breeze,
As each little poke brings giggles with ease.

They trade silly tales of their clumsy old names,
As the gnarly tree nods, it knows all their games.
With every odd verse, laughter fills up the air,
Turning frowns into chuckles, heaps of joy to share.

And when twilight beckons, and shadows take flight,
The bards leave the thorns in a jolly delight.
For beneath that old tree, laughter's never done,
In a place where the thorns help craft tales full of fun.

## Sonnet of the Stolen Bloom

In gardens grand, a flower bright,
I nicked it swift, oh what a sight!
It danced and twirled, with petals fair,
Now who will know? No one will care!

But from my pocket, it did peek,
With winks and sprigs, it tried to speak.
'You thief!' it squealed, with rosy pout,
'I'll have my revenge, just wait it out!'

In every vase, it seems to wilt,
All my mischief done with guilt.
Yet laughter blooms from every joke,
A heist so grand, my laughter woke!

So here I stand, a thief of cheer,
With stolen laughs, no need to fear.
A stolen bloom, a chuckle shared,
In every petal, funny tales prepared.

## Verses from the Brambles

Within the thicket, grins abound,
A mischievous sprite, I twirl around.
Thorns like daggers, sharp and spry,
Tickle my toes, oh me, oh my!

I pet the bushes, give them names,
'What's up, prickles? Any new games?'
They rattle back, with quite a jest,
'Alas! Too sharp for these poor pests!'

But lo, a berry, bright and sweet,
I plucked it fast, a tasty treat.
Yet in a twist, it shot my face,
Sweet and sour, oh, what a race!

Now here I sit, a jammed delight,
With bramble giggles, through the night.
A thorny tale, a prank so bold,
In laughter's arms, we all grow old.

## The Enchanted Quill


With quill in hand, I scribble mad,
My tales of woe, both good and bad.
It scratched my head, then laughed aloud,
'You silly bard, don't be too proud!'

Across the page, the ink does slide,
Writing of roses, with thorns as guide.
'Stop prancing words, get to the fun!'
It curtsy spins, 'I'm not yet done!'

Each word a tickle, each rhyme a whiff,
A playful poke, a literary gift.
But lo! It morphed into a beast,
Chasing me with a paper feast!

With frenzy danced, I dashed away,
My trusty quill now in dismay.
Yet laughter bloomed among the chase,
A tale untouched, in playful grace.

## Thorns That Sing

Oh, thorns that chirp, such silly sounds,
Do serenade through bumpy grounds.
They hum a tune, a wacky jig,
As I skip past, doing a big twig!

In shadows cast, a melody echoes,
With swaying branches, joy it bestows.
'Twist and turn!' they gently tease,
'Join the dance, oh please, oh please!'

Out comes the moon, to waltz with glee,
While thorns entwine, and sing to me.
A prickly embrace, a joyful sting,
With laughter's breeze, my heart takes wing!

So heed this tune, a quirky score,
From prickly friends, you can't ignore.
In every note, a jest unfurled,
In thorny smiles, a funny world.

## The Ballad of Bane and Beauty

In a realm where jests unfold,
Lived a bard with tales, quite bold.
A thorny crown upon his head,
He sang of love and folks misled.

With laughter echoing through the night,
His songs took flight like kites in light.
Each jest a poke, each word a tease,
His audience fell, as they'd wheeze and wheeze.

In gardens where the roses prance,
He danced around, a comic chance.
The thorns would prick, but oh so slight,
He winked and chuckled, all was right.

So raise a glass to laughter's art,
For beauty found in every part.
With every note and every grin,
A thorny tale ends with a spin.

## Secrets Perched on Hidden Daggers

Underneath the velvet skies,
Whispers float with playful lies.
A dagger's shine, a secret's thrill,
The jesters plot with joyous skill.

Each word a dance, a clever twist,
In shadows where the giggles persist.
A velvet glove conceals the blade,
In laughter's arms, their plans are laid.

Between the cracks of sunny cheer,
Lurk secrets sharp, yet oh so dear.
A smirk, a jest, a playful nudge,
Through thorns and laughs, they'll never budge.

So tip your hat to those who play,
With hidden blades, they light the way.
In a world where giggles reign,
Each secret tells of thorny gain.

## **Melodic Cuts, Rhythmic Thorns**

A bard with a harp, and thorns that sing,
Strummed melodies, oh what a fling!
Each note a jab, but wrapped in glee,
The audience danced, quite wild and free.

With fingers swift on strings they flew,
Each rhythmic pulse, a pointed cue.
For every jest, a jagged cheer,
In harmony's grip, they shed a tear.

Chasing laughs from dark to bright,
His melodies took merry flight.
A thorn might prick, but hearts would swell,
In playful tunes, they'd all rebel.

So let us sing of sharp delight,
In melodies that spark each night.
For life's a song, both fun and thorny,
In every cut, there lies a story.

## The Weave of Joy and Jaggedness

In a tapestry of laughs and sighs,
Stitched with tales and playful cries.
Joy woven tight with jagged thread,
A raucous rhyme where giggles spread.

A weaver's hand with cunning craft,
Mixed joy and thorns, a quilt quite daft.
Each stitch reveals a twist of fate,
As laughter bubbles, never late.

In every fold, a story spun,
A playful jab, and then a pun.
With each new row, the laughter swells,
In jagged cloth, the joy compels.

So let the laughter take its form,
In joyous weave, we all transform.
For life is sharper than we know,
In jagged joy, the heart shall glow.

www.ingramcontent.com/pod-product-compliance
Lightning Source LLC
Chambersburg PA
CBHW072128070526
44585CB00016B/1570